ARCHAEOLOGIST

By William David Thomas

Reading Consultant: Susan Nations, M.Ed.,
author/literacy coach/consultant in literacy development

Gareth Stevens
Publishing

Please visit our web site at **www.garethstevens.com.**
For a free catalog describing Gareth Stevens Publishing's list of high-quality books,
call 1-800-542-2595 (USA) or 1-800-387-3178 (Canada).
Gareth Stevens Publishing's fax: 1-877-542-2596

Library of Congress Cataloging-in-Publication Data
Thomas, William David.
    Archaeologist / by William David Thomas ; reading consultant: Susan Nations.
        p. cm. — (Cool careers : on the go)
    Includes bibliographical references and index.
    ISBN-13: 978-1-4339-0000-6 (lib. bdg.)   ISBN-10: 1-4339-0000-9 (lib. bdg.)
    ISBN-13: 978-1-4339-0164-5 (softcover)   ISBN-10: 1-4339-0164-1 (softcover)
    1. Archaeologists—Juvenile literature. 2. Archaeology—Juvenile literature.
I. Nations, Susan. II. Title.
CC107.T47   2009
930.1—dc22   2008024627

This edition first published in 2009 by
Gareth Stevens Publishing
A Weekly Reader® Company
1 Reader's Digest Rd.
Pleasantville, NY 10570-7000 USA

Copyright © 2009 by Gareth Stevens, Inc.

Executive Managing Editor: Lisa M. Herrington
Creative Director: Lisa Donovan
Editor: Joann Jovinelly
Designer: Paula Jo Smith
Photo Researcher: Kimberly Babbitt
Publisher: Keith Garton

Picture credits: Cover and title page: p. 5 Paramount/courtesy Everett Collection; p. 6
David Gallimore/Alamy; p. 7 Atlantide Phototravel/Corbis; p. 8 Tim Wright/Corbis; pp. 11,
12, 13 Shutterstock; p. 14 Emory Kristof/National Geographic; p. 16 Jim Sugar/Corbis; p. 17
RF/Getty Images; p. 18 Natalie Forbes/Corbis; p. 20 Todd Muskopf/Alamy; p. 21 Jonathan
Blair/Corbis; p. 23 Bojan Brecelj/Corbis; p. 24 Bridgeman Art Library/Getty Images; p. 25
Courtesy of LouAnn Wurst; p. 27 Christie's Images/Corbis; p. 28 Richard T. Nowitz/Corbis

Printed in the United States of America

1 2 3 4 5 6 7 8 9 10 09 08

CONTENTS

Words in the glossary appear in **bold** type the first time they are used in the text.

CHAPTER 1

SEARCHING FOR ANSWERS

With his old brown hat and bullwhip, Indiana Jones may be the world's most famous **archaeologist**. Near the end of his new adventure, he stands inside an ancient temple. Glass skeletons are all around him. Next, the bad guys show up, led by the beautiful but evil Irina Spalko. She points a gun at Jones. Spalko demands that he answer her questions. She shouts, "You've spent your whole life searching for answers!"

Spalko is right. Searching for answers is what archaeologists do. Finding those answers is an exciting job.

What Do Archaeologists Do?

Archaeologists study the past. They search for answers to questions about people who lived long ago. How did they build their homes? What tools did they use? What did they eat? What was their religion?

To find answers, archaeologists look for places where people lived in the past. These places are

Actors Harrison Ford and Shia LeBeouf check an archaeological site in the 2008 film, *Indiana Jones and the Kingdom of the Crystal Skull*.

called **sites**. There, archaeologists look for **artifacts**, or objects made by people long ago. Underground artifacts must be dug up. This process is called **excavation**. Archaeologists usually say they are "on a dig." Some sites are underwater. Objects must be brought up from beneath the water. All artifacts are cleaned, labeled, and tested. Then they can be studied.

Do Crystal Skulls Exist?

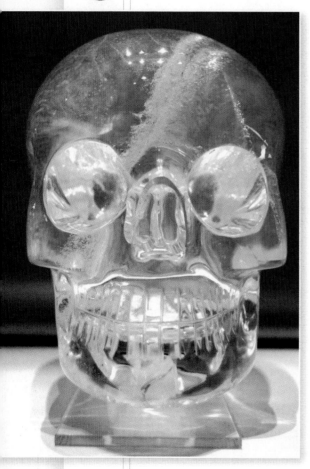

A crystal skull is a big part of the latest Indiana Jones movie. Crystal skulls do exist. Archaeologists once believed that the Maya people of South America carved the skulls more than 500 years ago. Today's archaeologists question that idea. New tests show that the skulls could not have been created so long ago. In fact, scientists think that they were carved in the 1900s. They studied the skulls under a special microscope. Scientists saw markings that could have been made only with modern tools.

Where Do Archaeologists Work?

Archaeologists work all over the world. They dig on mountains, in deserts, in jungles, and beneath oceans. They also dig in cities, towns, and empty fields. Many teach at colleges. Others work in libraries and museums. Some work in high-tech labs.

A dig takes place at a Native American site in Colorado. The strings and red flags help the archaeologists record the exact location of things they find.

How to Become an Archaeologist

If you want to become an archaeologist, you should have a curious mind. Most archaeologists have always wondered about the past. You should also like school. All archaeologists have bachelor's degrees. That takes four years of college. Most archaeologists have advanced degrees. That means another two to six years of study.

Slowly and carefully, these student archaeologists excavate a site at Jamestown, Virginia. It was first settled by English pioneers in 1607.

A lot of training takes place outdoors, not in a classroom. Students work at field sites. They are taught how to plan and do excavations. They learn to keep careful records about the objects they find. Students also learn what those objects can tell them about ancient people.

Is Archaeology Right for You?

If you think you'd like to be an archaeologist, ask yourself these questions:

- Are you interested in history?
- Do you have a lot of patience?
- Do you pay close attention to details?
- Would you like to visit foreign countries?
- Do you like working outdoors?

If so, archaeology may be the right career for you!

Try It Out!

Do you want to give archaeology a try? Many colleges, museums, and local parks have archaeology camps. The National Parks Service has summer digs just for kids. At these camps, kids work with real archaeologists. They learn what archaeologists do — and get to try it themselves!

CHAPTER 2
HOW ARCHAEOLOGISTS FIND SITES

When archaeologists want to find artifacts, where do they go? How do they know where to look? There are several ways that archaeologists find sites. One way is by reading **legends** and stories about the past. Another way is by searching areas that have a known link to the past. Some people might even find sites by sheer luck! Usually, though, archaeologists combine several methods. They also use high-tech tools to help them search.

Lost City Found

American explorer Hiram Bingham loved adventure. He was curious about the once-mighty Inca Empire. He read letters and reports about the Inca that were 200 years old. They told of a lost city in the mountains of Peru. Bingham wanted to find it.

In 1911, Bingham took his third trip to South America. He went to Peru. He walked through jungles and climbed high into the Andes Mountains. Finally, Bingham found the city. It was below a steep cliff. The city was nearly covered by forest. Bingham was one of the first explorers to see the city known as Machu Picchu (MAH-choo PEE-choo).

Clouds and mist swirl above the ruins of Machu Picchu, high in the mountains of Peru.

Who Were the Incas?

The Incas ruled one of the largest empires in South America from about 1200 to the mid-1500s. Their empire extended from present-day Colombia into western Argentina. When Hiram Bingham discovered Machu Picchu, he thought he had found the birthplace of the Inca Empire. Archaeologists have since learned that the city was a summer home for Incan kings.

Archaeologists have studied the mysteries of Stonehenge for years.

Mysterious Circle of Stones

Archaeologists also revisit known dig sites. Sometimes, they search old **ruins**. For example, Stonehenge is a circle of large stones in southwestern England. It was built about 4,600 years ago. Archaeologists have studied the site for years, but they still find new things there. In 2006, archaeologists found the remains of ancient houses nearby. They are still looking for more clues. In 2008, archaeologists announced that Stonehenge was likely an ancient burial site.

Ancient Cliff City

Many dig sites are found through patience and hard work. Sometimes, people find them by accident. In 1888, two cowboys were riding their horses in the mountains

of Colorado. They were looking for stray cattle. They rode into a snowy canyon called Mesa Verde. They looked up and saw a city of stone houses built into the canyon walls. In 1891, a Swedish archaeologist studied Mesa Verde. He learned that the Anasazi (ah-nuh-SAH-zee), an ancient tribe of Native Americans, had built the city. Since 1906, Mesa Verde has been protected as a national park.

The round structures at Mesa Verde are called kiva. They were used for religious meetings.

Finding the *Titanic*

Some archaeologists explore underwater. The ocean liner *Titanic* was said to be "unsinkable." But on its very first voyage, in 1912, the *Titanic* hit an iceberg and sank. More than 1,500 people died. For many years, people searched for the wreck, but no one could find it. Ocean explorer Robert Ballard tried and failed. Finally, he used a search ship with computers and **sonar**. Sonar uses sound waves to locate objects underwater. Ballard also used small robot submarines with lights and cameras. In 1985, he found the *Titanic's* wreck deep beneath the sea. It was about 1,000 miles (1,609 kilometers) east of Boston, Massachusetts.

Sonar helped explorer Robert Ballard discover the *Titanic* in 1985.

High-Tech Tools

Finding dig sites is hard work. Archaeologists have some high-tech tools to help them.

- **Ground Radar:** These instruments send sound waves into the ground. The waves bounce back if they hit a solid object.

- **Satellite Photographs:** Satellite images taken from space show things that cannot be seen from the ground. Satellite images can show the course of ancient rivers or where walls once stood.

- **Heat Scanners:** These scanners show images of temperature. Warm objects, such as sand or trees, show up in yellow or orange. Cooler objects, like the stones from old buildings, show up in blue or green.

- **Robots and Sonar:** Robots with cameras can go deep into the ocean. Sonar, like radar, sends out sound waves, but it works underwater. When the sound waves hit something, they bounce back. The waves make a picture on a screen only if they strike an object.

Thrill of It All

Hiram Bingham searched mountains and found a lost city. Robert Ballard searched an ocean and found a famous lost ship. The excitement of finding lost things keeps archaeologists working. They never know what they will find!

CHAPTER 3

TIME TO EXCAVATE

Archaeologists look for things that will tell them about the people who once lived at the site. They look for features and artifacts. Features are large, human-made objects. They may be as big as a pyramid or a building. They may also be the remains of a stone wall or a fireplace. Artifacts are smaller objects that people have left behind. Axes, coins, pots, clothes, and arrowheads are artifacts. Artifacts may even be the remains of people, such as skeletons or mummies.

An archaeologist excavates a skeleton thought to be about 2,000 years old. It was found in England.

When covered with dirt, these animal carvings could be mistaken for stones. Archaeologists must work slowly and carefully to find artifacts like these.

Archaeologists also look for links between objects. If they find a knife with pottery and animal bones, they may guess that the site was a kitchen. A knife found with arrows and spears might mean the site was a battleground.

On the Job: Arrowhead Archaeology

Larry Lahren is an archaeologist who lives in Montana. He has been digging up Native American artifacts since the 1960s. Lahren studies arrowheads and tools that he finds near his home. "Archaeologists try to get into the minds and technology of the past peoples," he told *Archaeology News*.

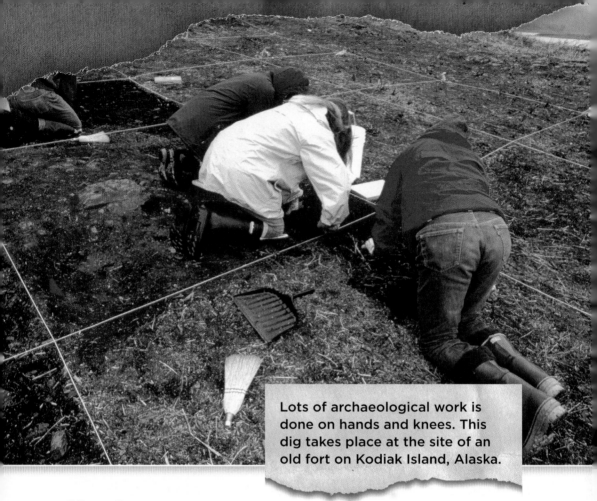

Lots of archaeological work is done on hands and knees. This dig takes place at the site of an old fort on Kodiak Island, Alaska.

Site Survey

Before they dig, archaeologists do a **site survey**. They walk slowly around the area, looking at it carefully. They may see some broken pottery on top of the ground. A mound of soil may have something beneath it.

Places to dig are marked with small flags. At each flagged place, archaeologists make a grid. It is a set of strings tied to pegs. The grid divides the site into squares, like a checkerboard. Excavation begins inside one square of the grid.

Excavation

Excavation is hard work. It often requires that archaeologists work on their hands and knees. They dig with hand tools such as shovels, **trowels**, and rakes.

When they find a large object, they use shovels and brushes to carefully remove the soil around and below it. Many artifacts break easily. Archaeologists want to keep them in one piece whenever they can.

Archaeologists use screen boxes to find small objects in soil. They place the dirt in the box. Then they gently shake the box back and forth. Dirt falls through the screen. Small artifacts, such as pieces of pottery, metal, or bones, are trapped above the screen.

Archaeologists number and label all artifacts they find. They may photograph the objects or sketch them in a notebook. Archaeologists take notes about exactly where each artifact was found. Then they carefully pack each piece for shipment.

Big City Dig

In 1893, about 27 million people went to the World's Fair in Chicago, Illinois. The fairground was called the "White City." Today, only one of the buildings is left standing. Archaeologists are looking for remains of the others. The dig site is right in the middle of one of the biggest cities in the United States!

Early American Archaeology

Colonial Williamsburg is in Virginia. The town was first settled in 1699. Today it has been restored. It is a "living museum." You can see people working as they did long ago. Many of the tools they use were found on the site by archaeologists. Excavations are still going on at Williamsburg. In the summer, you can watch the work. You can also visit a lab where artifacts are cleaned and tested.

These students really "dig" Colonial Williamsburg. The work requires patience, attention to detail, and good recordkeeping.

A grid helps this diver track items found on a shipwreck off the coast of Turkey.

Working Underwater

Underwater archaeology is similar to the study of artifacts on land. If the water is not very deep, divers can do a site survey. They may carry sonar gear or metal detectors to find objects under the seafloor. The divers use small plastic flags to mark places to work.

Divers then build underwater grids from metal rods or rope. They need special tools to work underwater. Instead of shovels, divers use **blowers** to uncover artifacts. Those tools blow air to move away **silt** on the seafloor. Special suction tubes, like big vacuum cleaners, suck up silt and soil. They trap solid objects in a fine screen.

Cold water protects materials, such as wood, that would be ruined underground. When artifacts are brought up to the surface, they must remain in water. Artifacts found under the seafloor must be dried slowly or they will be damaged.

CHAPTER 4

STUDYING THE PAST

When excavation is finished, there is more to do. Digging is only part of the job. Archaeologists must identify each object. They must also record their findings and **preserve** the artifacts.

Dating Objects

Part of the process is dating, or finding the age of artifacts. Archaeologists use several methods.

- **Sequencing:** This process puts items in order by age. Archaeologists can tell when one object is older than another. They compare items to similar artifacts that have already been dated.

- **Carbon-14 Dating:** All living things contain an element called **carbon-14**. When something dies, the carbon-14 begins to disappear. Archaeologists can measure how much carbon-14 is left. Then they can tell the age of an object.

- **Heat and Light Dating:** Archaeologists heat pieces of pottery to find the age of the items. When the pieces are very hot, they give off light as energy. That amount of energy can be measured. Then, using math, archaeologists can find the age of the pottery. Some archaeologists specialize in dating artifacts

Do you like jigsaw puzzles? An archaeologist sorts pieces from more than 100 different glasses, jugs, and plates. Careful records and testing help him tell which pieces go together.

and recording their findings. They do this work in high-tech laboratories. They pay attention to every detail.

Tests, Records, and Reports

Archaeologists also use chemicals to test artifacts. Chemical testing may tell what kind of metal was used to make a tool. Other items, such as cloth or pottery, may be looked at under a microscope. They may be X-rayed, too.

Sometimes archaeologists get help from other professionals. **Geologists** study rocks and the history of Earth. They may help identify stones found at sites.

Anthropologists study people's customs and beliefs. For example, if a carved figure is found at a dig site, an anthropologist can tell more about how it was used.

No project is finished until the paperwork is done. Archaeologists keep detailed records and reports. They **catalog**, or list, every artifact they find. Many people want to know what was found on a dig.

Secrets of King Tut

In the 1920s, many people became interested in archaeology. That was because of a unique discovery in Egypt. In 1922, archaeologist Howard Carter discovered an untouched tomb. It belonged to Tutankhamen, the boy king known as King Tut. Inside the tomb, Carter found hundreds of priceless artifacts. He also found King Tut's mummy! Years later, scientists X-rayed the mummy. Special scans showed that Tut probably died from an infection caused by a broken leg.

On the Job:
Archaeologist LouAnn Wurst

Archaeologist LouAnn Wurst teaches at the State University of New York College at Brockport, New York.

Q: When did you get interested in archaeology?

Wurst: I wanted to become an archaeologist since I was a kid. My mother was very interested in it, and I got hooked.

Q: What is the best thing about being an archaeologist?

Wurst: It is hard physical work that makes you sweat, but also hard mental work that makes you think. I like the combination.

Q: What part of archaeology do you like most?

Wurst: I love to dig sites, but I'm always glad when the season is over. I love to teach but am always happy when the semester ends. I love to do lab work but am always happy when the artifacts are all cataloged. I never do the same things long enough to get tired of them!

Q: Where have you gone on digs?

Wurst: A castle in Jordan; Roman ruins in Tunisia; a medieval city in India; and a whaling station site in Alaska.

Q: What would you tell young people who are thinking about a career in archaeology?

Wurst: Digging is only a small part of what we do. For each season we spend digging, it takes several years to catalog, identify, analyze, and write up our findings. Archaeology as shown on TV and films is just not real. What archaeologists actually do is much better!

CHAPTER 5

SOLVING MYSTERIES

Archaeologists like to solve mysteries about the past. After digging up the answers, they like to share what they have learned.

Some of them do this by helping to preserve ancient features. Visitors come from all countries to see the pyramids and Sphinx in Egypt. Tourists also visit the Aztec ruins in Mexico. In Italy, tourists can see the Coliseum, where gladiators fought. Archaeologists help set up these sites. They also work to protect them.

Books and Classrooms

One way archaeologists share what they learn is by writing about it. Many write books or magazine articles about their work. Some have their own web sites. Others teach at colleges. They help students learn how people lived in the past. Teachers may take their classes on excavations.

The Sphinx, in Egypt, is more than 4,600 years old. It is one of the world's most famous artifacts. A temple once stood between its paws.

Museums

Most artifacts found by archaeologists are sent to museums. Museum **curators** care for those artifacts. Curators choose which artifacts to display. They might group related artifacts together.

On the Job: Egypt Expert

Caroline Rocheleau is an archaeologist. She has worked on dig sites in Africa and in the Middle East. Now Caroline works as a curator in a museum in Raleigh, North Carolina. She is an expert on ancient Egypt. "I was only 9 years old," she says, "when I made a trip to Egypt with my parents. I sat near the entrance [to a pyramid], filling my pockets with pebbles. I still have those pebbles."

The way artifacts are displayed helps people understand why the items are important. Curators want museum visitors to learn about discoveries in archaeology. They want people to share in the excitement that archaeologists feel when they make a discovery.

A museum curator studies a sword that belonged to George Washington.

Career Fact File

ARCHAEOLOGIST

OUTLOOK

- The United States had about 2,800 archaeologists in 2006. By 2016, there will be jobs for about 3,200.
- Most archaeologists work for private companies, colleges, universities, or the U.S. government.

WHAT YOU'LL DO

- Archaeologists find and study materials that tell about people who lived long ago. These materials include ruins of buildings, tools, pottery, and even bones. From these items, archaeologists learn about the history, customs, and way of life of earlier times.

- Some archaeologists work in the field, finding and excavating ancient villages or towns. They may have to learn foreign languages, live in poor conditions, and do hard physical work.

- Other archaeologists work in labs that test and catalog materials found at field sites. Archaeologists also teach at colleges or museums and write about their findings. Many archaeologists combine those activities.

WHAT YOU'LL NEED

- All archaeologists must complete four years of college. Most go on for two to three more years to get master's degrees. Some continue to study to earn a doctoral degree.

WHAT YOU'LL EARN

- Archaeologists earn between $29,000 and $81,500 a year.

Source: U.S. Department of Labor, Bureau of Labor Statistics

GLOSSARY

anthropologists — scientists who study people, their beliefs, and their ways of life

archaeologist — a scientist who studies artifacts to learn how people lived long ago

artifacts — small objects made by people who lived long ago

blowers — machines that blow air to clear away dirt that may cover artifacts underwater

carbon-14 — an element that provides an accurate way to find the age of human, plant, or animal artifacts

catalog — to list and describe the artifacts found on a dig

curators — people who care for objects and display them in a museum

excavation — the process of uncovering something by digging in the ground

geologists — scientists who study the rocks and minerals that make up Earth

legends — very old stories that may or may not be true

preserve — to keep from being lost, damaged, or forgotten

ruins — the remains of something that was destroyed or has fallen apart from age

silt — fine particles of dirt or mud

sites — in archaeology, places where artifacts are found

site survey — the detailed examination and marking of an area before archaeologists begin to dig

sonar — an instrument that uses radio waves to find objects underwater

trowels — small hand tools with wide, flat triangular blades

TO FIND OUT MORE

Books

Archaeology. Kingfisher Knowledge (series). Trevor Barnes and
    Tony Robinson (Kingfisher Publishing, 2007)

Archaeology: Discovering the Past. John Orna-Ornstein
    (Oxford University Press, 2002)

Mesa Verde. Excavating the Past (series). Mary Quigley
    (Heinemann Library, 2005)

Stonehenge. The Unexplained (series). Matt Doeden
    (Edge Books, 2007)

Web Sites

Archaeology at Colonial Williamsburg
research.history.org/Archaeological_Research/KidsPage.cfm
    See artifacts left by kids 200 years ago and much more.

Dig! The Archaeology Magazine for Kids
www.digonsite.com
    Read articles and stories, and find links to more information.

National Geographic Archaeology News
news.nationalgeographic.com/news/archaeology.html
    Learn about new finds and digs.

National Park Service — Archaeology Programs for Kids
www.nps.gov/history/archeology/public/kids/index.htm
    Check out special archaeology summer programs for students.

Underwater Archaeology
www.underwaterarchaeology.com
    Get "below the surface" of archaeology news!

INDEX

About the Author

William David Thomas lives in Rochester, New York. In his career, Bill has written software documentation, magazine articles, training programs, annual reports, books for children, speeches, a few poems, and lots of letters. Bill claims he was once the King of Fiji but gave up the throne to pursue a career as a relief pitcher. It's not true.